Community Helpers

Police
Officers

by Cari Meister

Bullfrog
Books

Ideas for Parents and Teachers

Bullfrog Books let children practice reading informational text at the earliest reading levels. Repetition, familiar words, and photo labels support early readers.

Before Reading
- Discuss the cover photo. What does it tell them?
- Look at the picture glossary together. Read and discuss the words.

Read the Book
- "Walk" through the book and look at the photos. Let the child ask questions. Point out the photo labels.
- Read the book to the child, or have him or her read independently.

After Reading
- Prompt the child to think more. Ask: Where have you seen a police officer? What was he or she doing? What kind of things could a police officer help you with?

Bullfrog Books are published by Jump!
5357 Penn Avenue South
Minneapolis, MN 55419
www.jumplibrary.com

Library of Congress Cataloging-in-Publication Data
Meister, Cari.
  Police officers / by Cari Meister.
    pages cm. — (Bullfrog books : Community helpers)
  Includes bibliographical references and index.
  Summary: "This photo-illustrated book for early readers gives examples of how police officers fight crime and keep people safe" — Provided by publisher.
  ISBN 978-1-62031-078-6 (hardcover : alk. paper) —
  ISBN 978-1-62031-444-9 (paperback) —
  ISBN 978-1-62496-034-5 (ebook)
  1. Police — Juvenile literature. I. Title.
  HV7922.M43 2014
  363.2'3—dc23
                                    2012044153

Series Editor: Rebecca Glaser
Series Designer: Ellen Huber
Book Designer: Lindaanne Donohoe

Photo Credits: Alamy, cover, 4, 14–15; Lindaanne Donohoe, 1; Corbis, 18–19; iStockPhoto, 10, 11, 21, 23br; Shutterstock, 3, 5, 6–7, 8–9, 12, 13, 16, 17, 20, 22, 23tl, 23bl, 23tr, 24

Printed in the United States of America at Corporate Graphics in North Mankato, Minnesota.

Table of Contents

Police Officers at Work

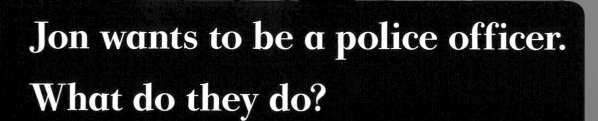

Jon wants to be a police officer.
What do they do?

They keep people safe.

They make sure people follow laws.

Officer Brown works in the city.

He rides a bike.

He looks for danger.

Officer Beck patrols the roads.

Amy is going too fast.

He pulls her over.

She gets a speeding ticket.

speeding ticket

Max is a police dog.
He has a great sense of smell.

12

He helps
find criminals.

Oh no!

A car crash!

Officer Rex rushes over.

He helps.

A man robbed a bank.

Police chase him.

They put handcuffs on him.

handcuffs

Officer Lee is at school.

She tells kids how to be safe.

Police officers do good work!

At the Police Station

computer
Police officers use computers to keep track of crime reports.

chief of police
The police officer who is the boss.

radio
A device that allows police officers to talk with each other.

Picture Glossary

criminal
A person who breaks a law.

patrol
To travel around an area to keep watch on it and make sure people are safe.

handcuffs
A metal locking device put around a person's wrists.

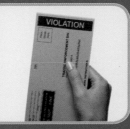

speeding ticket
A ticket given by a police officer if a person is driving too fast; the driver has to pay a fine.

Index

To Learn More

Learning more is as easy as 1, 2, 3.

1) Go to www.factsurfer.com

2) Enter "police officer" into the search box.

3) Click the "Surf" button to see a list of websites.

With factsurfer.com, finding more information is just a click away.